PRIM'S MAGICAL POMP'S.

The Story of an Irish Dancer finding her feet...

Laureen Gallagher

Thank you to my mum for always believing in me and to my fiancé David I love you.

There was a little girl who dreamed of Irish dancing every night,

Miss Prim would close her eyes, and there she was on stage, standing in the light.

So off to her first Irish dance class
Prim was set to go,
Her mummy held her hand while
she showed her teacher how she
could point her toe.

Her fancy new pomps were her
new favourite shoes,
She was taught jump two 3s and
hop two 3s,
And a lot of other moves.

Her brand new Pomps were magic.

It was something she just knew,

She could get so tall on her tippy toes

And jump higher than all the older girls too.

Miss Thompson was her teacher, and it seemed like she was Prim's biggest fan,
She taught her all about competitions, wigs, and even putting on fake tan!

But Prim knew it was the magic
shoes, and this was a secret she
would keep,
Because these pomp's made her
Burl, rock and sometimes even leap.

At night she would hang up her pomp's next to her Irish dancing dress.

Her mummy got it for her first Feis, and she knew it would impress.

Her first feis day had arrived,
and she was in bed excited as she lay,
But when she turned to admire her sparkling dress
Prim notices her magic pomps were away!

She searched her room for her
pomp's but only found her poodle socks,

Her mummy told not to worry
as her new shoes were in the box.

Prim's eyes filled with tears and
she then began to cry,
She knew she wouldn't be as good,
and she wouldn't be able to jump as high.

She stood side stage, waiting to
dance with her tummy filled with nerves.

She just hoped she could dance
her best and get what she deserved.

As Prim took to the stage and
heard the reel music begin to play,
Her smile returned as her feet
took over and danced her steps
the right way.

She couldn't believe she did it, and Miss Thompson was so proud.

She pointed her toe, took a big bow and heard cheering from the crowd.

Her mummy then gave her a present and inside it can you guess?
It was her magic shoes that had now been blinged with jewels that carefully matched her dress.

She looked up to her Mummy, who
was standing proud,
Prim was excited and said aloud,

"Mummy, I thought my shoes were
magic, and I see now
that isn't true.

"Oh, What a beautiful Irish dancer
you are Prim, and my darling, that
is all down to **You**".

Printed in Great Britain
by Amazon